Fire Fighters
Community Workers

by Lucia Raatma

Content Adviser: Jeff Sedivec,
California State Firefighters' Association

Reading Adviser: Dr. Linda D. Labbo,
Department of Reading Education, College of Education,
The University of Georgia

COMPASS POINT BOOKS

Minneapolis, Minnesota

Compass Point Books
3722 West 50th Street, #115
Minneapolis, MN 55410

Visit Compass Point Books on the Internet at *www.compasspointbooks.com* or e-mail your
request to *custserv@compasspointbooks.com*

Photographs ©:

FPG International/Rob Gage, cover; Dembinsky Photo Assoc. Inc./John Mielcarek, 4; Dembinsky Photo Assoc. Inc./John Mielcarek,
6; Dembinsky Photo Assoc. Inc./John Mielcarek, 7; Dembinsky Photo Assoc. Inc./John Mielcarek, 8; Dembinsky Photo Assoc. Inc./
John Mielcarek, 9; International Stock/Andre Jenny, 10; FPG International/Ron Rovtar, 11; Kate Boykin, 12; FPG International/
Arthur Tilley, 13; William B. Folsom, 14; Dembinsky Photo Assoc. Inc./Claudia Adams, 15; FPG International/Jeffrey Silvester, 18;
Photo Network/Todd Powell, 20; Photri-Microstock/Harry Giglio, 22; Leslie O'Shaughnessy, 23; Dembinsky Photo Assoc. Inc./
Steven Frank, 24; Visuals Unlimited/Kevin and Betty Collins, 16; Photo Network/Bachmann, 17; Shaffer Photography/
James L. Shaffer, 19; Dembinsky Photo Assoc. Inc./John Mielcarek, 21; Dembinsky Photo Assoc. Inc./Jim Regan, 25;
Dembinsky Photo Assoc. Inc./M. L. Dembinsky, 26; International Stock/Phyllis Picardi, 27.

Editors: E. Russell Primm and Emily J. Dolbear
Photo Researcher: Svetlana Zhurkina
Photo Selector: Linda S. Koutris
Design: Bradfordesign, Inc.

Library of Congress Cataloging-in-Publication Data

Raatma, Lucia.
   Fire fighters / by Lucia Raatma.
     p. cm. — (Community workers)
   Includes bibliographical references and index.
   Summary: Introduces the job of fire fighter, including the duties, hazards, uniforms, equipment,
and contribution to the community.
   ISBN 0-7565-0009-5 (hard : libr. binding)
     1. Fire fighters—Juvenile literature. 2. Fire extinction—Juvenile literature. [1. Fire fighters.
2. Fire extinction. 3. Occupations.] I. Title. II. Series.
   TH9148 .R317 2000
   363.37'092—dc21
                                                 00-008625

Table of Contents

What Do Fire Fighters Do?

Fire fighters are brave people. They fight fires in homes and other buildings. People know they can count on fire fighters for help.

◀ Fire fighters use a ladder to rescue people in a tall building.

What Tools and Equipment Do They Use?

Fire trucks have ladders and hoses. Fire fighters use the ladders to reach people in high places. They use hoses to spray water on flames. Fire fighters hook their hoses to fire **hydrants** or water tanks.

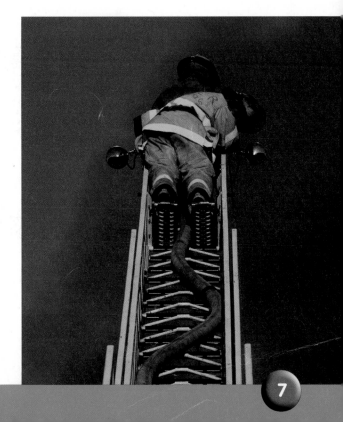

◀ Fire fighters open a fire hydrant.

A fire fighter carries a hose up a ladder. ▶

How Does a Fire Fighter Help?

Fire fighters help keep communities safe. Many lives are saved by fire fighters. People are lucky to have fire fighters to help them.

◄ Fire fighters save a woman from a building and help her down the ladder.

Fire fighters rescue people trapped in a car after an accident. ▶

Where Do They Work?

Some fire fighters work in city **fire stations**. Other fire fighters work in small towns, where they are called to help put out fires when they are needed. They are **volunteer fire fighters.**

◄ Fire trucks parked in a fire station

Fire fighters eat their meals at the fire station when they are on call. ►

Who Do They Work With?

Fire fighters work with the police. They also help medical workers when accidents happen. Sometimes fire fighters work with **fire inspectors**. They find out whether **criminals** set the fires.

◄ A fire department ambulance

A medical worker ▶ treats a girl at the scene of a fire.

What Do They Wear?

Fire fighters wear special clothing to protect them in a fire. This clothing does not catch fire. They also wear air tanks and masks to help them breathe. They need to get air without breathing in smoke.

A fire fighter checks his equipment.

Fire fighters sometimes wear masks to help them breathe.

What Training Does It Take?

People who want to be fire fighters must finish high school. They also must study science in school. People who want to be fire fighters have to be strong and healthy. They have to pass a fitness test. In the test, they have to run, climb, and jump.

◀ Volunteer fire fighters in training

A teacher checks a fire fighter's mask during training. ▶

What Skills Do They Need?

Fire fighters have to be able to follow orders. They work as a team to put out any fire. Fire fighters also have to be able to stay calm and act quickly when they are at a fire.

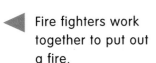
Fire fighters work together to put out a fire.

A commander gives orders.

What Problems Do They Face?

Fires are very dangerous. Fire fighters can be burned by the fires. They also can be hurt if they breathe in the smoke from fires.

◀ A fire fighter wears an oxygen tank in a burning house.

Fire fighters battle a large garbage fire at night. ▶

Every day, fire fighters risk their own lives to help others. Fire fighters often must search in dark and smoky hallways for people who need help. They can get trapped in a burning building.

◀ Fire fighters put out a fire at a warehouse.

Leaving a burning building ▶

Would You Like to Be a Fire Fighter?

Are you strong and healthy? Do you like working with others? Can you think quickly in scary situations? Maybe you would like to be a fire fighter someday. You can prepare now. In school, learn how to follow directions. Exercise. Practice working with others.

Schoolchildren on a trip to the fire station

A fire fighter shows a student how to use a fire extinguisher.

A Fire Fighter's Tools and Clothes

helmet

coat

glove

ax

boots

SQUAD 1

On the Fire Truck

siren

ladder

hose valve

rescue basket

A Fire Fighter's Day

Early morning
- The fire fighter arrives at the fire station for a twenty-four-hour day. First, the fire fighters meet to decide their jobs for the day.
- Then, they clean the fire house and do practice drills.

Noon
- The fire fighter makes lunch for the other fire fighters.
- After lunch, he cleans and repairs his equipment.

Afternoon
- When a call comes in, the fire fighter dresses quickly in his special clothing. He rides with other fire fighters on the truck.
- The fire fighter puts on his mask and air tank and looks for people in the burning building. He gives first aid to people who are hurt.
- Then, the fire fighter uses a hose to spray water on the building.

Evening
- After the fire is completely out, the fire fighters return to the fire station for dinner.

Night
- The fire fighter cleans up and tries to sleep before the next call.

Glossary

criminals—people who have broken the law

fire inspectors—fire fighters who study fires set by criminals

fire stations—buildings that hold fire trucks and fire fighters

hydrants—pipes on the street that carry water through hoses to put out fires

volunteer fire fighters—people who fight fires when they are needed and without pay

Did You Know?

- More than 280,000 men and women work as fire fighters in the United States.

- Benjamin Franklin started the first fire fighting company in Philadelphia in 1736.

- In colonial times, a chain of people passed buckets of water from hand to hand to put out fires.

- Nearly 31,000 people die in fires in the United States each year.

Want to Know More?

At the Library

Moignot, Daniel. *Fire Fighting*. New York: Scholastic, 1999.

Ready, Dee. *Fire Fighters*. Mankato, Minn.: Bridgestone Books, 1997.

Royston, Angela. *Fire Fighter!* New York: Dorling Kindersley, 2000.

On the Web

The Fire Fighters Memorial Web Site

http://www.fireengine.net/

A site that explores the history of fire fighting

Fire Prevention and Education

http://www.geocities.com/Athens/Academy/3483/index01/html

An informative site featuring all kinds of fire-safety tips

Through the Mail

International Association of Fire Fighters

1750 New York Avenue, N.W.

Washington, DC 20006

For information about a career as a fire fighter

On the Road

New York City Fire Museum

278 Spring Street

New York, NY 10013

212/691-1303

To see a rich history of fire fighting equipment in a 1904 building

Index

About the Author
Lucia Raatma received her bachelor's degree in English literature from the University of South Carolina and her master's degree in cinema studies from New York University. She has written a wide range of books for young people. When she is not researching or writing, she enjoys going to movies, playing tennis, and spending time with her husband, daughter, and golden retriever.